WHAT'S WRONG WITH BEING CRABBY?

Peanuts® Parade Paperbacks

WHAT'S WRONG WITH BEING CRABBY?

Cartoons from *Sunday's Fun Day, Charlie Brown*
and *As You Like It, Charlie Brown*

by Charles M. Schulz

Holt, Rinehart and Winston / New York

Published simultaneously in Canada by Holt, Rinehart
and Winston of Canada, Limited.

First published in this form in 1976.

Library of Congress Catalog Card Number: 75-29872

ISBN: 0-03-017486-4

Printed in the United States of America

10 9 8 7 6 5 4 3 2 1

AH! A PERFECT DAY!

ALL RIGHT, RISE AN' SHINE! IT'S RABBIT-CHASING TIME!!

OH, GOOD GRIEF!

THE SNOW IS FRESH AND THE AIR IS CLEAR...I PREDICT WE'LL SEE LOTS OF GAME!

HOW CAN YOU CHASE RABBITS IN THE MIDDLE OF THE NIGHT?

WELL START HERE...THIS IS A BIG FIELD, AND YOU SHOULD BE ABLE TO PICK UP THE SCENT WITHOUT...

Z

WAKE UP!

OKAY! HERE WE GO!!

SNIF SNIF SNIF SNIF

SNIF SNIF SNIF SNIF SNIF

I GUESS WERE NOT GOING TO FIND ANY, SNOOPY, BUT AT LEAST WE TRIED...

EVEN THOUGH YOU'VE FAILED, IT ALWAYS MAKES YOU FEEL BETTER WHEN YOU KNOW YOU'VE DONE YOUR BEST!

I'D HATE TO DISILLUSION HER, BUT I DON'T EVEN KNOW WHAT A RABBIT SMELLS LIKE!

SCHULZ

STUPID LEAVES!

ONE FINGER WILL MEAN A FAST BALL, TWO FINGERS A CURVE AND THREE FINGERS A SLOW BALL... OKAY?

FINE

WHAT WERE YOU TWO TALKING ABOUT?

WE WERE JUST DISCUSSING OUR SIGNALS

OH..

I THOUGHT MAYBE YOU WERE TALKING ABOUT **ME**...

I GUESS THAT'S UNDERSTANDABLE IF YOU'RE PARTICULARLY SENSITIVE!

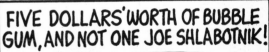

THERE'S NEVER ANYTHING TO DO!

I NEED SOMETHING TO CHALLENGE ME.. I NEED SOME NEW INTEREST...

IF YOU WANT A HOBBY, WHY DON'T YOU COLLECT LEAVES? YOU CAN PRESS THEM BETWEEN THE PAGES OF A BOOK..

THAT'S A WONDERFUL IDEA!

WHAP!

WELL, I DID IT! I'VE COLLECTED OVER A DOZEN DIFFERENT KINDS OF LEAVES!

MY ONLY PROBLEM CAME IN SELECTING WHAT SORT OF BOOK I SHOULD PRESS THEM IN..OF COURSE, I KNEW IT HAD TO BE A LARGE VOLUME...

I FIRST THOUGHT OF "THE DECLINE AND FALL OF THE ROMAN EMPIRE," AND THEN I CONSIDERED "LOOK HOMEWARD ANGEL," BUT I FINALLY DECIDED ON A VOLUME CALLED, "THE PROPHECIES OF DANIEL" BECAUSE I FELT THAT..

GET OUT OF HERE!

PEOPLE REALLY AREN'T INTERESTED IN HEARING YOU TALK ABOUT YOUR HOBBY..

GOLLY! HAVE YOU EVER SEEN SO MANY SNAKES AND LIZARDS IN ALL YOUR LIFE?!! NO...AND SPIDERS, TOO... SPIDERS, TOO? YEAH, SNAKES AND LIZARDS AND SPIDERS!

AND THEY'RE ALL HEADED THIS WAY, YOU SAY? YEAH, THERE'S A WHOLE FLOCK OF 'EM...ALL HEADED THIS WAY...CREEPING AND CRAWLING... SNAKES AN' LIZARDS AN'..

PTUI!

PTUI!

UNTIL IT IS DEMONSTRATED, ONE FORGETS THE REALLY GREAT DIFFERENCE THAT EXISTS BETWEEN THE MERELY COMPETENT AMATEUR AND THE VERY EXPERT PROFESSIONAL

IT'S STARTING TO RAIN, CHARLIE BROWN... AREN'T WE GOING TO CALL THE GAME?

NO, WE'RE NOT GOING TO CALL THE GAME, SO YOU MIGHT AS WELL GET BACK OUT THERE IN CENTER FIELD WHERE YOU BELONG!

AND TRY TO PAY ATTENTION TO WHAT YOU'RE DOING!

POW!

BONK

THIS IS GOING TO BE ANOTHER GREAT SEASON!

SCHULZ

SCHOOL ZONE

※ SIGH ※

THERE'S THAT LITTLE RED-HAIRED GIRL WALKING HOME FROM SCHOOL....JUST THINK... I'M WALKING ON THE SAME SIDEWALK SHE'S WALKING ON

OF COURSE, I'M WALKING SEVEN BLOCKS BEHIND HER, BUT I'M WALKING ON THE VERY SAME SIDEWALK

I WISH I WERE WALKING WITH HER...I WISH I WERE WALKING RIGHT BESIDE HER, AND WE WERE TALKING

SHE WENT INTO THAT NICE HOUSE! SO THAT'S WHERE SHE LIVES...AND THERE'S THE DOOR SHE WENT IN...

I WISH SHE'D INVITE ME OVER TO HER HOUSE SOME TIME.. I WISH SHE'D COME UP TO ME, AND SAY,"WHY DON'T YOU COME OVER TO MY HOUSE AFTER SCHOOL, CHARLIE BROWN?"

THERE SHE IS AGAIN..SHE WENT INTO THE BACK YARD, AND SHE'S SWINGING ON HER SWING-SET...

WE COULD WALK HOME FROM SCHOOL TOGETHER, AND THEN WE COULD SWING ON HER SWING-SET...

BOY, WHAT A BLOCKHEAD I AM! I'LL NEVER GET TO SWING WITH HER! I'LL NEVER GET TO WALK WITH HER! I'LL NEVER EVEN GET TO SAY ONE WORD TO HER!

ALL I GET TO DO IS WALK HOME FROM SCHOOL BY MYSELF, AND...

OH, HI, SNOOPY

YOU'RE NOT MUCH OF A SUBSTITUTE FOR A LITTLE RED-HAIRED GIRL

QUITE OFTEN LATELY I HAVE THE FEELING I DON'T KNOW WHAT'S GOING ON...

YOU KNOW...A PRINCESS SORT OF THING...A WHITE DRESS AND NICE SLIPPERS...

AND A BIG BALLROOM!

UH, HUH...

BUT I GUESS THAT'S KIND OF SILLY ISN'T IT, CHARLIE BROWN?

NO...OH, NO...NOT AT ALL...

I MEAN..WELL...WE ALL HAVE OUR LITTLE DAYDREAMS OR AMBITIONS OR WHATEVER YOU WANT TO CALL THEM..

I MEAN..THERE'S ONE I'VE HAD MYSELF FOR YEARS, BUT I'VE NEVER TOLD ANYONE..

WHAT, CHARLIE BROWN? YOU CAN TELL ME..

OH, NO...IT'S NOT THE SORT OF THING I SHOULD TELL...NO, I DON'T THINK I SHOULD...

OH, COME ON...I WOULDN'T GIVE IT AWAY..COME ON..

PLEASE?

WELL,...I'VE ALWAYS WANTED TO BE CALLED, "FLASH"... I HATE THE NAME, "CHARLIE"... I'D LIKE TO BE REAL ATHLETIC, AND HAVE EVERYBODY CALL ME, "FLASH".....I'D LIKE TO BE SO GOOD AT EVERYTHING THAT ALL AROUND SCHOOL I'D BE KNOWN AS "FLASH," AND...

HEY, VIOLET! LISTEN TO THIS!

"FLASH"?

"FLASH"! HA! HA! HA! HA! HA! HA! "FLASH" BROWN!! HA! HA! HA! HA!

I CAN'T STAND IT!

SCHULZ

Here it is!

SNOOPY, I'D LIKE TO READ YOU A STORY I'VE WRITTEN AND ILLUSTRATED FOR SCHOOL...

"ONCE THERE WAS A LITTLE GIRL WHO HAD A HEADACHE."

HER MOM GAVE HER SOME PILLS, BUT THEY DIDN'T HELP. HER MOM THEN TOOK HER TO THE DOCTOR.

"THE DOCTOR WAS UNABLE TO FIND ANYTHING WRONG."

"THIS IS A MYSTERIOUS CASE," HE SAID.

"THE LITTLE GIRL'S MOTHER TOOK HER HOME, AND PUT HER TO BED... HER HEAD THROBBED."

"HER LITTLE BROTHER CAME IN, AND SAID, 'MAYBE YOUR EARS ARE TOO TIGHT.'"

SO HE LOOSENED EACH EAR ONE TURN BACK. HER HEADACHE SUDDENLY STOPPED, AND SHE NEVER HAD ANOTHER HEADACHE AGAIN.

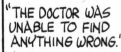

I GUESS HE DIDN'T LIKE IT.... THAT WAS HIS "GOOD LUCK, YOU'RE GOING TO NEED IT" HANDSHAKE!

WHAT IN THE WORLD ARE YOU DOING?

ONE MINUTE YOU'RE IN CENTER FIELD, AND THE NEXT MINUTE YOU'RE GONE! WHAT KIND OF BALL PLAYER ARE YOU?!!

I WAS STANDING OUT THERE IN CENTER FIELD, CHARLIE BROWN, AND I WAS PAYING ATTENTION LIKE YOU ALWAYS TELL ME TO DO..

SUDDENLY, OUT OF NOWHERE, I HEARD A PIECE OF CAKE CALLING ME!

I HATE IT WHEN THE BASEBALL SEASON IS OVER

THERE'S A DREARINESS IN THE AIR THAT DEPRESSES ME...

EVERYTHING SEEMS SAD...EVEN THE OL' PITCHER'S MOUND IS COVERED WITH WEEDS...

I GUESS ALL A PERSON CAN DO IS DREAM HIS DREAMS...MAYBE I'LL BE A GOOD BALL PLAYER SOMEDAY...MAYBE I'LL EVEN PLAY IN THE WORLD SERIES, AND BE A HERO...

?

I BET I WILL PLAY IN THE WORLD SERIES SOMEDAY...I BET I'LL...

HEY! LOOK WHO'S OUT HERE TALKING TO HIMSELF!

WHAT ARE YOU DOING, CHARLIE BROWN, THINKING ABOUT ALL THE TIMES YOU STRUCK OUT?!

THERE'S A DREARINESS IN THE AIR THAT DEPRESSES ME!

SCHULZ

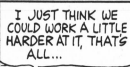

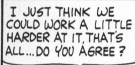

SCHULZ

HERE'S THE FIERCE MOUNTAIN LION WAITING FOR HIS VICTIM...

AUGH!

SOMEHOW MY ATTACKS ALWAYS SEEM TO LACK FORCE!

SCHULZ

I SUPPOSE YOU'RE ALL WONDERING WHY I'VE ASKED YOU HERE TODAY...

IF YOU THROW THAT SNOWBALL AT ME, I'LL HAVE THE HUMANE SOCIETY ON YOU SO FAST IT'LL MAKE YOUR HEAD SWIM!

WHOEVER PAINTS THOSE SIGNS FOR HIM, DOES A GOOD JOB!

- SCHULZ

SAY! I LIKE THAT CAP, LUCY!

THANK YOU..

YOU'RE ALL SET FOR COLD WEATHER, AREN'T YOU?

YES, I GUESS I AM..

YOU KNOW WHAT IT'S LIKE TO BE COLD AND UNCOMFORTABLE, DON'T YOU?

OH, YES...I KNOW THAT FEELING...

YOU LIKE ANIMALS, DON'T YOU? I MEAN, YOU'VE ALWAYS BEEN SORT OF AN ANIMAL LOVER, HAVEN'T YOU?

OF COURSE!

DOGS, TOO? ESPECIALLY DOGS WHO SLEEP OUTSIDE, AND SHIVER AND SHAKE ALL NIGHT?

✳SIGH✳

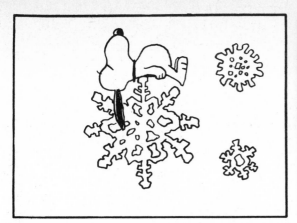

WHICH DO YOU WANT ME TO UNPLUG... THE TV OR YOUR CLOCK-RADIO?

Happiness is a Christmas vacation with no book reports to write.

DEAR SANTA CLAUS, HOW HAVE YOU BEEN?

PLEASE DON'T GET THE IDEA THAT I AM WRITING BECAUSE I WANT SOMETHING.

NOTHING COULD BE FURTHER FROM THE TRUTH. I WANT NOTHING.

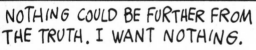

IF YOU WANT TO SKIP OUR HOUSE THIS YEAR, GO RIGHT AHEAD. I WON'T BE OFFENDED. REALLY I WON'T.

SPEND YOUR TIME ELSEWHERE. DON'T BOTHER WITH ME. I REALLY MEAN IT.

WHAT IN THE WORLD KIND OF LETTER IS THIS?!!

I'M HOPING THAT HE'LL FIND MY ATTITUDE PECULIARLY REFRESHING

SCHULZ

YOU WON'T DO IT, HUH?

NOPE!

I WANT PEOPLE TO HAVE MORE TO SAY ABOUT ME AFTER I'M GONE THAN, "HE WAS A NICE GUY... HE CHASED STICKS!"

AAUGH!

KLUNK

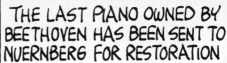

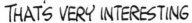

NEVER TRY TO PLAY JACKS ON A HOT SIDEWALK!

WHAT'S THE DATE TODAY?

TODAY IS THE SIXTEENTH..

I KNEW I HAD THE WRONG THUMB...

ON ODD DAYS I USE MY LEFT THUMB, AND ON EVEN DAYS I USE MY RIGHT THUMB!

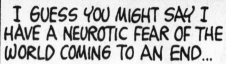

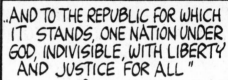

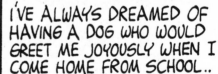

SNOOPY'S IN THE HOSPITAL?

UH HUH...DIDN'T YOU KNOW? HE'S BEEN THERE FOR ABOUT FOUR DAYS...

IS HE ALLOWED TO HAVE VISITORS?

OH, YES...HE'S HAD A FEW CLOSE FRIENDS DROP BY ALREADY...

WHAT ARE THEY DOING TO MAKE SNOOPY GET WELL, CHARLIE BROWN?

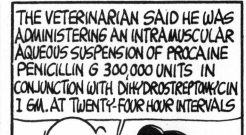

THE VETERINARIAN SAID HE WAS ADMINISTERING AN INTRAMUSCULAR AQUEOUS SUSPENSION OF PROCAINE PENICILLIN G 300,000 UNITS IN CONJUNCTION WITH DIHYDROSTREPTOMYCIN 1 GM. AT TWENTY-FOUR HOUR INTERVALS

OH...

DEAR SNOOPY,
I MISS YOU MORE THAN I CAN SAY.

I HOPE THEY ARE TREATING YOU WELL IN THE HOSPITAL.

WHILE YOU ARE THERE, WHY DON'T YOU HAVE THEM GIVE YOU A FLEA BATH?

I SAY THIS, OF COURSE, AT THE RISK OF BEING OFFENSIVE. HOPING TO SEE YOU SOON. YOUR PAL, CHARLIE BROWN

SUPPERTIME!

!

GOOD GRIEF! I KNEW HE WAS IN THE HOSPITAL...AND YET I FIXED HIS SUPPER...

HURRY HOME, SNOOPY... I'M CRACKING UP!

SNOOPY!

HAPPINESS IS COMING HOME FROM THE HOSPITAL!

THEY TREATED ME VERY WELL IN THE HOSPITAL..

I'LL ALWAYS BE GRATEFUL TO THEM...

I WILL SAY ONE THING, HOWEVER...

IT'S KIND OF NICE TO GET HOME TO YOUR OWN BED AGAIN!

YOUR NAME IS **WHAT?**

MY NAME IS "5"!

MY DAD SAYS WE HAVE SO MANY NUMBERS THESE DAYS WE'RE ALL LOSING OUR IDENTITY..

HE'S DECIDED THAT EVERYONE IN OUR FAMILY SHOULD HAVE A NUMBER INSTEAD OF A NAME

CHARLIE BROWN, I'D LIKE TO HAVE YOU MEET 5!

OH NO!

OUR FAMILY NAME IS 95472.. ACTUALLY THAT'S OUR ZIP CODE NUMBER...

IN FACT, THAT WAS THE NUMBER THAT SORT OF STARTED THE WHOLE THING...THAT WAS THE NUMBER THAT FINALLY CAUSED MY DAD TO BECOME COMPLETELY HYSTERICAL ONE NIGHT

MY FULL NAME IS 555 95472, BUT EVERYONE CALLS ME 5 FOR SHORT....I HAVE TWO SISTERS NAMED 3 AND 4

THOSE ARE NICE FEMININE NAMES...

WE THINK SO

SCHULZ

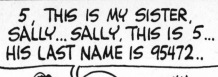

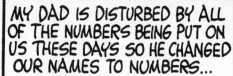

SO WHAT'S THERE TO DO THE **REST** OF THE DAY?

NOBODY LIKES ME...EVERYBODY HATES ME...

WELL, CHARLIE BROWN, IF THE WHOLE WORLD IS EVER AGAINST YOU, I'D LIKE TO HAVE YOU KNOW HOW I'LL FEEL...

WILL YOU BE MY FRIEND?

NO, I'LL BE AGAINST YOU, TOO!

DON'T TELL ME YOU'RE SITTING HERE WAITING FOR THE "GREAT PUMPKIN" AGAIN?

HOW CAN YOU BELIEVE IN SOMETHING THAT JUST ISN'T TRUE? HE'S NEVER GOING TO SHOW UP! HE DOESN'T EXIST!

WHEN YOU STOP BELIEVING IN THAT FELLOW WITH THE RED SUIT AND WHITE BEARD WHO GOES, "HO HO HO", I'LL STOP BELIEVING IN THE "GREAT PUMPKIN"!

WE ARE OBVIOUSLY SEPARATED BY DENOMINATIONAL DIFFERENCES!

HE KNOWS WHICH KIDS HAVE BEEN GOOD AND WHICH KIDS HAVE BEEN BAD...

AND ON HALLOWEEN NIGHT THE "GREAT PUMPKIN" RISES OUT OF THE PUMPKIN PATCH, AND FLIES THROUGH THE AIR WITH HIS BAG OF TOYS FOR ALL THE GOOD CHILDREN IN THE WORLD!

HOW LONG HAS IT BEEN SINCE YOU'VE HAD A PHYSICAL CHECK-UP?

WELL, HOW DID IT GO LAST NIGHT?

NOT SO GOOD...I SAT OUT THERE UNTIL FOUR O'CLOCK IN THE MORNING, BUT THE "GREAT PUMPKIN" NEVER CAME...I ALMOST FROZE TO DEATH..

I GUESS A PUMPKIN PATCH CAN BE PRETTY COLD AT FOUR IN THE MORNING..

ESPECIALLY WHEN IT HAS BEEN CHILLED WITH DISAPPOINTMENT

OH "GREAT PUMPKIN," YOU'VE LET ME DOWN AGAIN!

I'LL NEVER BELIEVE IN YOU AGAIN! NEVER!

DON'T LISTEN TO ME..I DON'T KNOW WHAT I'M SAYING!

I HEAR THE PRICE OF HAIRCUTS MAY GO UP AGAIN..

YES, ISN'T THAT GREAT?! THEN MY DAD CAN BUY FOUR NEW CARS, A SWIMMING POOL AND A STABLE OF RIDING HORSES!

WE CAN EAT STEAK EVERY NIGHT, AND SPEND ALL OUR WINTERS ON THE RIVIERA!

I NEVER KNEW A BARBER'S SON COULD BE SO SARCASTIC..

MY DAD IS STILL WORRIED ABOUT THE PRICE OF HAIRCUTS..

HE'S THREATENING AGAIN TO BUY ONE OF THOSE KITS, AND CUT MY HAIR HIMSELF

THAT'S A GOOD IDEA...AND WHILE YOU'RE AT IT WHY DON'T YOU WRITE YOUR OWN BOOKS, PAINT YOUR OWN PAINTINGS AND COMPOSE YOUR OWN MUSIC?

I NEVER REALIZED THAT BARBERS' SONS WERE SO SENSITIVE...

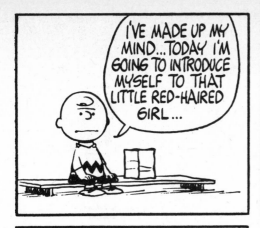

DEAR SANTA, HERE IS A LIST OF WHAT I WANT.

HOW DO YOU SUPPOSE SANTA CLAUS CAN AFFORD TO GIVE AWAY ALL THOSE TOYS?

PROMOTION! DON'T KID YOURSELF.... EVERYTHING THESE DAYS IS PROMOTION!

I'LL BET IF THE TRUTH WERE BROUGHT OUT, YOU'D FIND THAT HE'S BEING FINANCED BY SOME BIG EASTERN CHAIN!

LUCY SAYS THAT SANTA CLAUS IS CONTROLLED BY SOME BIG EASTERN SYNDICATE...

DON'T BELIEVE HER.. THAT'S THE SORT OF STORY THAT GOES AROUND EVERY YEAR AT THIS TIME...

TAKE IT FROM ME.. HE'S CLEAN!

BLEAH!

DEAR SANTA CLAUS,
I AM WRITING IN BEHALF OF MY DOG, SNOOPY. HE IS A GOOD DOG.

IN FACT, I'LL BET IF ONE OF YOUR REINDEER EVER GOT SICK, SNOOPY WOULD FILL IN FOR HIM, AND HELP PULL YOUR SLED.

AHEM!

WELL, PERHAPS NOT. BUT HE'S STILL A GOOD DOG IN MANY WAYS.

GOOD GRIEF!

MONDAY IS BEETHOVEN'S BIRTHDAY!

HAVE A GOOD TIME!

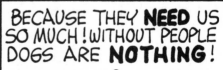
I GUESS SOMEBODY'S GETTING HUNGRY!

DO YOU KNOW WHY DOGS LIKE PEOPLE?

BECAUSE THEY **NEED** US SO MUCH! WITHOUT PEOPLE DOGS ARE **NOTHING**!

I THOUGHT I'D BETTER LEAVE BEFORE I BEGAN BITING A FEW APPROPRIATE LEGS..

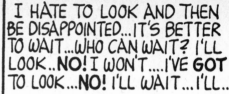

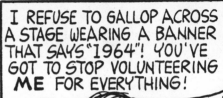

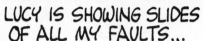

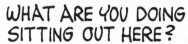

"AN UNJUST KING ASKED A HOLY MAN, 'WHAT IS MORE EXCELLENT THAN PRAYER?'"

"THE HOLY MAN SAID: 'FOR YOU TO REMAIN ASLEEP TILL MIDDAY, THAT FOR THIS ONE INTERVAL YOU MAY NOT AFFLICT MANKIND.'"

BACK TO BED!

BOOT!

HUMANE SOCIETY

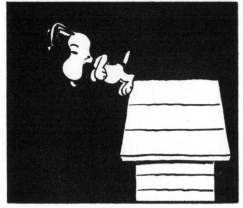

DID YOU HEAR THAT? MY TEACHER SAID, "GOOD MORNING" TO ME!

NOW, I WONDER WHAT SHE MEANT BY THAT? DID SHE REALLY MEAN TO WISH ME "GOOD MORNING"? MAYBE SHE WAS BEING SARCASTIC...

MAYBE SHE WAS TRYING TO TEACH ME TO BE POLITE... MAYBE SHE THOUGHT SOMEONE FROM THE SCHOOL BOARD WAS LISTENING..

MAYBE WHEN I MEET HER IN THE HALL, IT WOULD BE BEST TO LOOK THE OTHER WAY..

I GUESS I HAVE TO GO TO THE BARBER SHOP..

DO YOU THINK I NEED A HAIRCUT?

YES, I THINK YOU DO... YOUR HAIR IS PRETTY LONG...

IF IT GETS ANY LONGER, YOU'LL BE ABLE TO BUTTON IT!

SCHULZ

PTUI!

CHARLIE BROWN, THAT LITTLE RED-HAIRED GIRL WANTS YOU TO COME OVER, AND EAT LUNCH WITH HER..

APRIL FOOL!

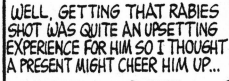

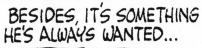

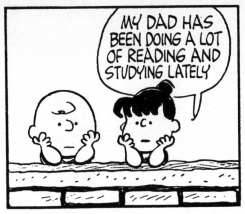

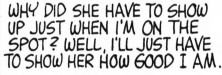